December 26 to Christmas

Poetry on the Everlasting Gift

by

Joe Bisicchia

Acknowledgements

for the manuscript

December 26 to Christmas

"Merry Christmas! — published in *Edify*, 2017

"Sighting at a Stop Light" — published in *Edify*, 2017

"Merriment, Our Love" — published in *Edify*, 2017

"Sighting in Hot Texas" — published by *Underwood Press - True Chili*, 2021

"Black Nazarene" — published in *Ancient Paths*, 2022

"May You See It Sit" — published in *Cacti Fur*, 2023

Contents

December 26

Santa Claus
has long left the building.
How quickly spins away
a nimbus?
But what of today?
What of the day next?
What may stay,
simply, every day
as Christmas?
As if here, not distant.
As if next week,
and next month,
and forever subsequent.
Connecting all effervescence,
its existence,
this passing Christmas,
never passing away.
Let it stay, as if
by Love's very nature,
Love shall always descend
to be with us.
With us, yes, *with* us.
So much in the preposition.
Love embraces the word.
As if INRI, and arms extend
again and again,
Christmas, this day,
paradise, with us,
no matter the present day.

Present

It is a box from above.
Not emptiness.
But what always is.
Unwrapped, it manifests.
The greatest everyday gift.
Love, in its presence.
Here, amidst us.
So it is, every moment,
Christmas.

Hallelujah Echoes

Joy to the world!

Round and round.

How wide must a heart open
for that joy to fit?

Worldwide, for just a start.

Easily done, for the open heart
has the breadth of infinity to it.

Evergreen

Not a lingering past,
even if indeed it sprouts
all the ages now into the bygone.
Not a dying leaf on a tired, worn branch,
finally falling, but aimlessly lost.
Rather simply one of trust.
Of belief.
That life and love is this way evergreen.

And we may now just run like a rabbit.
Soar the wide opened sky like a gull.
Ever free in our amazing machinery.

Or, better yet, stay all this while here.
With our voices of Christmas cheer.
Not calling out for Jesus Barabbas,
but for the true Son of the Father.
With melody of heart-song
even in the supposed silence of night,
even in the supposed silence of light,
the ongoing awakening flicker,
the past, present and future.

Not just a dream.
Not just a Christmas tree.
But timelessness of togetherness.

This is our now.

And we now know forever to last,
as we welcome the presence as present,
the star atop the lights,
the sound of this.
With us, all around.

Our Noel

Blinking lights
and the steady beam
strand like arteries
known by heart,
cascading from high star.

And we are,
as we colour the evergreen
ours.

It does not only belong to us,
this tree, this time, this noel.

Nothing to fear,
with awe of heaven here.

In the midst of this,
near and far,
no matter where we are,
the song of our collective soul,
in this way as always is,
never truly alone,
all because of Christmas.

Sometimes the Clock

Stops.
Steps aside.
Time does.

This is more than time.

Sound the silver bells
as if no matter the concern,
heaven must be clearly heard.

Time can only then jingle,
jingle,
even when life fails to rhyme.

And this can be anywhere
and everywhere.
For time has no place
for getting in the way.

Christmas Truce, 1914

No matter the time of the year,
we should think of peace
and how to welcome it here.

Ever deep within respective trench,
may it last, our humanity.
May songs sung mix well the air.

Of our differences,
so much more is same.
Now and through the ages.

Let us sketch the enduring redbreast,
not by bayonet,
but of the mindset of cheer.

Let us share beer, tins of beef and jam,
and make it last beyond no man's land.
Beyond today's ever too soon sunset.

Long from now and every day hence,
each of us may reminisce all of this
as Christmas.

And by grace, know it as still here
ever willing within, no matter the place
and no matter the time of the year.

Beyond Bethlehem

What shall be left of the star
after it dissipates?

How long
will the seraphim and cherubim
and their hallelujah songs persist?

How swift is an age, but
what endlessly stays?

What day of heaven shall come
and remain as if in timelessness?

What day of mercy, of forgiveness
seventy times seven and ever more,
will be set in place?

What is not fantasy, but reality
in all the straw of the never-ending,
not hidden under all the wrapping?

Love surely must outlast all there is.

But, where is the peace we pray?

O, that we may still look outward
and yet be beckoned by grace
to find what is now hallowed here,

the ongoing source of joy for all of us,
wherever we are, face to face.
All because of what has happened,
and happens every day,
as Christmas.

So Much Seems to End

And so again,
we sing our Christmases
and sing all our passwords
memorized for a time
and maybe soon forgotten,
soon packed away
with the wishing tree.

Still,
life's ornaments might dangle
somehow instead
like lost poems in our heads,
like lost opportunities
if only to beckon again.
Or, to be remembered again
in that meteoric moment
just before
a grown up child falls asleep.

Or, like sunrise, to be found
just over the bend where
grace patiently again waits.

May You See It Sit

And may you not miss it
like you did this past Christmas,
and somehow even year round,
in the pear tree, the partridge.

That is, if only,
such a sitting bird
would have time
for such a seat to find
so to help an eyewitness.

Meantime,
time is swiftly time. And
soon enough
you see the pear tree again bend
suddenly,
and then at the bouncing branch
all is empty with nothing to see.

Yes, time flies.
Such a cliché.

But open the eyes, at the heart.
And soon again,
you shall see,
if only you believe,
to know and to see Love,
ever perched,

and to just let it gloriously be
that which stays
despite all that flies away.

Confetti upon the Nativity

Amidst all the past,
amidst all the new,
this happy new year,
we find ourselves here.

Near as Corinthians.
As written,
so we fix our eyes
not on what is seen,
but on what is unseen.

We are here and all is a blur.
The swirl.
Ephemeral.
We are here, and yet,
all that is unseen is eternal.

All of us in this living room.
Blinding disarray.
The moment. Here.
The New Year. Indeed, see.
Kiss to kiss to kiss to kiss.

Facing my deceased father
in my teenaged son
as our cheeks at first miss

but then we connect
to this

presence

of forever.

everyday miracles

with more than our fill
of provided figgy pudding
another egg nog and now
a visit under mistletoe and
then we can even later laugh

at how funny a new pup is
at first oblivious then
welcoming the expected
to her image in our mirror
as she eats from her dish

and I like how you talk
to the fish as you feed them
and the tree reflects its
lights upon the glass
and we kiss to remember

how we had first met
a face finding a face
that moment of seeing
a familiar grace
as if no happenstance

Manner of This Day

We've had better days than January's
when journeys start, and yet feel like an end.
But still, here we are as survivors, our eyes
like this upon each other's and all is new
to begin yet again. And this is true.

If living is the cause of death, there is more
to living, and it never ends. And so live we do.
We live the year our canvas, and it is Day 1.
We live in the city, and drift here to this room.
You feed the fish, and put on a reindeer sweater.
And one also for the pup. And we rush outside
to stand in a crowd of the living.

Broad this street for so many funeral parlors
end to end as a New Year's parade passes,
it does with sequins, and meets all of the city
with sun at our backs. Even as we stand still,
we chase the future as if our shadows are each
a daffodil in a field of daffodils to reach.

Loud the city hall clock reminds, and the year
shall pass. But, like the city tree that sleeps,
burrows deep underneath its concrete dreams
of leaves, we along with life are peace. We
blush in from the banjos of the street.

And this very day, despite how cold outside,
January paints so much like heaven, and here
we are fashioning spring but patient, for now
has its place. Let now breathe, and let now
breathe again. We are the present in between.

Today in a Bow

Every day glows
of Christmas
in a bow.

Yes, even today.

A new baby,
a learned lullaby,
a first day of school,
a new bike.

Buds new upon the tree,
then crimson red leaves.
A life well worn.

A newness,
even in the change,
even in the mundane,
even in the dullest of days.
Yes, and even
a new way of seeing
the routine gratefully
as never before seen.

It is meant to be lived,
the gold, frankincense,
and myrrh to give.

Love is that gift.

And with it, this day.

This,
the wise by grace bestow
ever generous,
giving Love this day,
the best of themselves
wrapped in a bow,
whatever this day shall be.

Every Day

God is love.

Time for a timeless gift
to receive and to give,
more valuable
than any frankincense.

And that is simply this:
the ability to *see*
and the ability to *be*
the love that God is.

Black Nazarene

You are far more than make believe,
far more than wood portrayed in suffering,
but the divine embodiment here amidst humanity.
And You make Your way.

You choose, You do, this way of thirst, to carry it,
the cross. You bare Your soul along our streets
through every Quiapo, on the way to crucifixion
seemingly day after day.

Even here, now. Your devotees opine in prayer
and look up to You. You, carved from mesquite,
robed in red sovereignty, hair braided of dyed abaca,
and halo, a golden crown.

And You are far more than this parade.
You are far more than any image, any charade.
Far more than any nativity infant figurine, handmade.
You are real. You are Love.

You, they know. The Filipino knows the passion
and suffering. The cross thou hadst died upon,
very emblem of their salvation. Only wood upon
wood, some may say, having fallen here,

having fallen to Manila via galleon centuries ago,
having fallen to humankind.
But this much we all may know—
this creation of Eden that You so very well carry,

this weight You bear as we all now look up
at You, is simply for all of us. Now, and always.
And in us, for us, the world, You spring forth Love.
For this, You thirst. For this You rise. For each

and every one of us.
Not because of any righteous ritual on humanity's part.
But by Your mercy. And we of humanity joyfully sing.
Oh, Nazarine, we glorify thee!

Taking Down the Decorations

But,
weren't we just putting them up?
Now back into the boxes, and
I still see the colors in you.

Even now as you pass the vacuum.
And all that confetti far and wide
still hides deep into the carpet.

Stuck, stubborn bits and pieces stay.

So much disappears. But,
so much is left to tug and
to live its never-ending way.

Best of all, we are still here too.
And, here comes Valentine.
Long after the Mistletoe.

Buffalo Snow

Maybe it is lake effect, or a sound effect
or maybe just a side effect of what is arranged
as winter.
Silence seems at first a paralysis,
as if fear has frozen us all as Christmas passes.

But if ears dare to open, inward sings the ongoing
Niagara. It runs not so far from here.
Still, it too, is wont to go seemingly still
as if what runs in all of us is not far, but here.
Near as the blurred heart runs in place.

We have faults, and another hard winter ahead,
we fear. Hard, and sharp, then numb to the ear,
numb to the land now hammered to skin, a silence.
And winter seems an immovable stone.

But not to the soul which forever moves.
Listen to the soul float softly at peace, like garland
slipping to floor off the living room evergreen
now fading. And the coffee is now percolating.

And Nat King Cole is now crooning. And
this present and future ahead is ahead for us all
in the unending lifespan of a soul. We breathe in
this moment, this melt, for all our joys run
to glisten in lights again, all our silent nights
up and down our plowed and salted roads.

Angels We Have Heard

Boiler utters its gust to the new day.
We may want to believe in angels
under the stairs. Final frontier
may be the distance here to there.

You say, listen to the angels!
And to remember thankfulness.

You say,
be grateful for all we now possess
of this vanishing day.

You say, toss away any selfishness,
for selfishness only burns our mirrors,
obliterates that which was not so lovely
in the first place.

And then, you say, let us close our eyes
and wash the face. Feel the fresh tap
of faith warm and cozy
like a persistent February,
long past Christmas, but worthy
of a hot tea to start the day.

And be grateful.

And I say, yes, I am so very blessed
to be with such an angel.

Spirit of Christmas

Time came and went, if even ever begun.
Might just be dreaming this,
   this very missed Merry Christmas,
this midnight pa rum pum pum pum.

            Like an ongoing, steady,
steady and sweet-sounding
                  pa rum pum pum pum.

What an amazement, the heart.

All yuletide icons must surely glisten
as we all may listen for sirens
this very missed Merry Christmas.

Hope has a way of sometimes hiding.
Or by us being somewhere shoved aside.
And then rising with the angels.

Right now in hospitals across the globe
linger those in a coma, in a burn unit,
off the grid maybe by a twisted sleigh,
a wreck, here to the tree line
amidst all the needles of evergreen,
to a hospital bed.

Lights may dangle, may dim, but
never diminish this spirit.
So goes hope.

After all, in this mist, it lives
                    no matter what date
      near as the lights
strung by angels, still lit.

To all the world from Bethlehem,
we pray for them, those who are hurting.
And those caring for them.

Pale Pumpkin

Such a short month, and yet, it's only still February. We had our long fall, long ago, or just a while, and since then the groundhog has slept. Rodent might rise to see Jack O Lantern still smile. Yes, still. So much has past. So much snow, with so much coldness to go. Earth dies behind the shed and dies again as time mixes. And the pumpkin carcass sits and looks up at narrowing sky as if a zombie amidst all the old reappearing leathered leaves, coffee grinds, broccoli stems and the dead. And the shed itself dies, for its walls are eaten a bit, but survives our recent times, the hardest of which, this past Christmas without him.

And yet, back here behind the shed, with snow shovels standing, we try to uncover our brother in our own way when we finally unravel the stiff tar paper he had promised to use so to wrap the family fig tree as he always did. But with all the sorrowful madness, that wrapping never took place, and the tree was left out in the cold with all our frozen memories. But, if not too late, and by the good Lord's grace we'll finally wrap it now for the sake of its roots.

And then fittingly, little Susie hums *O Tannenbaum*. She and her big brother always hummed that song together while putting up the Christmas tree, the one that this past year never came out of its box. We join in, of course, because we can hear him hum along.

March Onward

In like the lion,
as if by Good Friday nails,
nipped in the bud,
the blossoms suffer
shortness of breath,
hope fallen at our doorstep.

But beyond our skin,
remains what is hidden.

Of our depth's warmth,
will we be kind?
Will we be children enough
to believe enough
to love enough
to understand?

Of the frost,
of the cross of each
crystallized line,
will we still find time
to give in to faith
so to arise from death
and woolen our flowers
up and out like the lamb?

Spring Snow

They drove here together.
Not expecting the suddenness
of weather, but it happens.
Even now, so close to Easter.

Outside, all had been dry.
Until the first reading inside.
Such things happen.
All the time.

Outside the stained glass
everything is now white. Inside,
like every star upon her hand,
life is authentic in her melt.

There is the sign of the peace.
A gentle kiss upon the cheek.
A gratefulness to be here.
A readiness for what shall be.

She smiles and knows so soon
the swift sky shall move beyond
even June to forever. Lord knows.
Santa knows it all. Yesterday

he held her in his arms and sang
lullabies. And now here again,
this Palm Sunday, he walks
with his daughter to communion.

She sees him, beyond his cancer.
How soon he has become old.
Time goes by, like timing belts,
the tuna melts, and the dissolve

of snow now upon their smiles
as they walk through the white,
resurrecting winters of the past,
as simply now.

Shared Landscape

Christmas is always right around the bend,
so bound to happen for household names,
for the countless, each counted and known,
loved and at home, as all the world should be.

Jesus and we now sit for another new supper,
celebratory in our same joy. Skin of earth,
cardboard. Corrugated in its tissue. Here
in city park under tree where we share ribs
from biodegradable carton, the reclaimed
marrow from garbage bin on this his birthday
no less, we think, no, yes, today Christmas.
After all, sudden slew of flakes fall upon us
a thundersnow. And, so, we ponder it confetti
for the passing anniversary, if it is to pass.
That said, how special it is that he stays.

Blessed, we count upward the few leaves
weathering the cold. Here we are underneath
pallor of this salted sky, now all of us another
day closer to old, falling only to quickly melt.

After words, the mountain is steep, but we
treat it like a hill, somewhat of a glistening,
luxurious imaginary leather sofa seat. For
those untested to such frill, we can share the
way of the world. To do that, this is critical—
we become like golden maple leaves, and fall

asleep upon these layers of cardboard, fetal
under falling heaven, new as newborns.

Together, we share a peace of the ever so far
yet near silvery sky as it descends to earth
between the bent branches all the way down
to here. We allow ourselves dignity, for sky
knows us as we are, loves us as we are, as it
reaches down to our level and kisses our
childlike faces, sauced red by the bare bones.

Merry Christmas, and it is, as Jesus gives
up all of heaven for this, almost homeless.

Easter Egg Hunt in the Living Room

And so goes C Street like Christmas.
We wrap our things and we laugh
at our apparent impermanence
and finally realize now is forever.

Out in the rain, rose petals are unravelling.
And the tulips are curtseying. And we
have surely ended our indomitable ice age.
There is a lasting life in here. It rolls onward.

There is Christmas even in this moment,
a sense of presence as if, yes, life is.
For, as it is, like the rolled away stone,
our hearts open infinite abundance of room.

We thank God that God is not an atheist
as we walk the hardwood as if saplings
flickering our new arms through the sun.
And despite empty branches, we see green.

And so even beyond the dead of winter,
now the distant past, there is bloom. Here
in this living room of now, spring's luster.
What is buried is buried, but not the ladder.

That which is life always rises its spirit.
Is what is ongoing and has no end, but is.
Today we shimmer our Easter and
begin again sharing the love we now are.

An overflowing 12 baskets
from the Easter Bunny, as if there is one.
We'll settle for the good Lord instead.
After all, who else would raise the dead?

Circle the Date

In the milky sky,
a circle of suspected sorrow,
the sun.

Tomorrow, it shall hide
and leaves shall surrender
and all the trees shall freeze,
save the evergreen.

But tomorrow
is not always what it seems to be
today.

To get to tomorrow,
we need to make our way
through today.

And why not continue today
what has begun?

All of it so blessed.

After all,
we had a Christmas dinner
full of love today.

Just like yesterday.

Even though, it's only May.

May Is Too Soon a Memory

O, the burst that is and soon was,
so addicting spring's fleeting flare.
Like the vibrant lights in a flicker
so quickly off the Christmas tree,
the twinkle darkens away.

In all that is temporary, beware
we may lose sight of the light
and what is so simply beautiful
in every unfathomable soul.
O, the burst that is, ever within.

In a Blink

And the world
goes round.
Sooner or later

full circle we'll know
our daily walls of Jericho
fall at more than a horn.

Love
goes round the world,
here to there, there to here.

See our tree blink
Christmas
to Christmas,

present
to
present,

again, even now.

All the colors within.

May Moves

And maybe therein
our old Christmas blues.

For too easily
what remains we lose,

morning to mourning,
mourning to morning,

and the new day's glory
soon goes noon.

We hold our breath
and yet

the breeze
shall leave.

Red goes the azalea
so soon just green.

Just ourselves.

To June.

Before Commencement

The long academic robes had long marched by him. So much has passed by since he first walked here. Long after birds knew flight and stones flew angrily over walls and gyms were built multipurpose for basketballs and then also for graduations for when it suddenly rains outside and sky goes predictably gravitational and academic places are unable to hold down educated people, so they say, long after the first full bladder, it has now lifted to this. An old janitor fetches his ladder to fetch the stubborn runaway 2. And that's why right now, he's thinking about Christmas.

Time always seems to be a runaway. That balloon with the orderly number has now fluttered up there to be stuck to a beam, leaving us it would seem in the first millennium even though it's a modern day auditorium arisen long after the elderly John Glenn and other jetted beings, and long after so many, so many, so many stars, so many, yet always like the same star dusted off and hoisted into place atop this janitor's particular family Christmas tree, the small artificial one now boxed, every ready, in his own home attic afar.

While steady now atop ladder he takes the number and brings down the 2. And audience applauds the scene and his 42 forever years as he'll soon be finally retiring end of June. But not yet.

Life's march has a patience to it. A letting go. Life's march has a stick-to-it-iveness. A holding on. All along, the ever envisioning of a star's positioning. He puts back this year's digits temporarily into place, and up again is the 2 like the star on his Christmas tree.

And all is right for him, again properly in order. Over two thousand years, and it all still is quite beautiful. Time is this type of march. Soon the procession, and the pomp and circumstances. He is just beginning. For the time being, he puts away the ladder.

Merry 4th

We may move slow but
we finally see eye to eye
our plastic reindeer, two by two,
their stiff legs upright, and even
Rudolph doesn't put up a fight.

All of them with faded complexion,
long bleached by summer sun.

Now, finally, the herd can welcome
the shade, and with thuds
they're back into the shed.

Merry Christmas!

There's joy in believing in an Unending Being,
loving enough to be human being, heaven sharing.

All year long.

Maybe it's a talking point to think of that
even while stuck in summer traffic to the shore.

And then, when finally there by the sea,
seeing the ocean tide toward you reach.
Oh tidings of comfort and joy.
Comfort and joy.

Sighting at a Stop Light

We saw Santa this summer
 on a motorcycle.
    Like us, he was stopped at a new red.
Impressive how he seemed the patient fellow.

        Dasher, Dancer, Prancer, and the rest
had just plowed through yellow.
Guess they were rushing to get to the beach.
And Santa smiled at us a Christmas scene.

We waved and waved,
and clapped in between.
    Then we were on our merry way
            when light turned green.

Foofaraw in the Woods

We overzealous campers
twirled and swirled
the garland and the tinsel
and, thinking it Christmas,
realizing then again
at the tangled trail twisted,
it only being still summer,
sensed something different
to this.

And the captured Bigfoot
seemed at first embarrassed
to these developments,
but then rather relieved
finally found,
as if all discoveries
are tightly wrapped in bows.

And we all exchanged gifts.

Lasting Whiff of Home

That smell of offal,
like who knows what, just tripe.
And we nearly lose ourselves,
our fingers in the diced onions
and in the greasy peppers,
the night of the weary.

Old Advent candles remain lit,
the saving power in each wick.
Teary the eyes like steamed glass,
like a tulip near the door
wanting to run away, only to stay
ready for this, but with a wilt.

Remembrance of Christmas
and the staying power of things,
the fragrance of the evergreen,
all so soon to eventually dissipate.

But, then again, the seven fish,
a lasting fist, is never fast to scatter,
as if, still here, now even in summer.
Yes, its own garlands of Christmas
somehow stubbornly stick to this place
long after the long gone taste.

And, still, the kitchen knows to whirl
yet again
as if all the year was made of even this.

No surprise.
It's our ever sweet sustenance
circling amidst the range's mist,
the aroma of our togetherness,
just like Christmas.

It's simply us being us.

Mark Your Calendar

Today.

Rise.

And fall in love

like Christmas morning.

Do.

Soon
the day will be.

As every day.

Merriment, Our Love

And so it is, finally July 25.

Feel the tide arise like eyes arriving to a party,
and like Christmas lights strung the whole way
from street to stairs to all the way up here
to where the disco ball rotates above hardwood

and the ballroom somehow feels like something
maybe from an old black and white movie,
sans the ambiguous grays, and the lost olden days,
for this is our newlywed first dance and evergreen.

The prism stays when the charism is from within,
and we walk on water in love, this our first spin.
And I feel like every Adam ever did, loving Eve,
and thinking no one else ever could love like this.

And every day onward, so it is.
Just like Christmas.

Sighting in Hot Texas

Goodness, not what we've expected here
at this roadside barbecue. A surprise,
not so much the old bearded man
flipping the burgers. Nor reindeer playing
reindeer games. But Mrs. Claus is a soprano.

She sings *White Christmas*
and other snowy things in sun's heat.
How lovely it bellows, her musical dream,
as if the future is now, as if now goes
through here, a united getaway
on a shared journey.

Her melody lofts over the smoking ribs,
the corn on the cobb, and watermelon too.
And she sings in tune perfectly. Seems
all seasons, always now, a flawless time
for such wintry reverie.

Might have to join her
and sing our cowboy dreams right along.
Now it's *Silver Bells* and
we're ringing in the peaceful twilight,
ever cool, and tossing horse shoes as well.
With the affable elves.

Christmas in Our Jalopy

It may be July
and hot as hell,
but Daddy opens the door

and he proudly hangs the little tree
air freshener, now dangling.
And Mommy cheerfully breathes.

And for the moment
we're not homeless
any more.

Taste of Water

And so soon to now,
in the wide melt,
the Christmas white
high upon the mountains
has dissolved down our sides
to here, in this roar.
We are as we are.

The gutters run down the street.
And afterward,
our summer stockings are hung
by our dormant chimneys with care.
Blessed are we in the thaw
to receive our necessities,
like socks, in the least,
to be filled with our wet feet.

And to drink.

And every day,
for so many of us,
our flasks shall overflow
with the little things
that mean so much.

In the cloudburst and rivers
subsequent, the presents
upon presents
shall flavor our lives with life.

And so, we offer all the water
to the world.

Sad if we dry our eyes
and our hearts as well
to those who,
for such simple presence,
still thirst.

Like Christmas

eyes out there go blind
like the missing stars
or the lonely dime
out there maybe unseen
but may you dream
of here
this hot griddle morning
on some table
may you come to mind
at the colorful plastic tree
with half bagel and
somehow some coffee
rather than tossed aside
may you find
it is surely kind inside
behind such a big sign
this welcome sign
Grace's Diner
yes
you are welcome here
clear as day
clear as that big sign
even if only a soup kitchen
with all the angels here
decorated as elves
you recognize them all
each for who they are
for their name
is on the big sign

Evergreen Aside the Highway

Seasons run in a blur.
Radio speaks again in circles
our new day rush and hush
as evergreen to the side stands brunt
yet again against the autumn wind.
We go in tin can cars
as the night dies as dawn begins.

We hang ornaments upon ourselves
and string our lights.
We move and move each of us,
swift as Christmas.
Big as sky is colorful, small as eyes
freshly awake to squint.
Harsh white can be the horizon.
But again we go.

And as we make our way, soon
this evergreen muscles the snow.
Its arms bend. Its peak reaches.
And we go.

Our new day hush, each of us
in the rush,
within our various siloes.
Winter comes and goes,
along with our armored clothes.

We pass the spring, and
the summer evergreen,
as it is.

A reminder of who we each are.

Me and My Teddy Bear

On this porch swing, looking out to everything,
you like it when we sing for all of autumn.
You hold me, and I hold you, near as now.

There is so much comfort in the very moment.
As known by all saints and indeed all souls,
that in the gold of every leaf, joy springs.

It is why every angel sings,
even if so much gets lost in the scattered leaves
despite the songs of us heard in the breeze.

So much is also found, and so we sing along.
Yes, you and me, we have a way of believing.
Seeing all around us, all the present splendor.

Tidings of comfort and joy, comfort and joy!
Yes, we sing wide like angels at Christmas,
on this porch swing, looking out to everything.

October

We turn our leaves
and might masquerade.
Time taketh so much away.
Might seem to leave little.
Yet, our wealth gains.
Lord giveth, overflowing.

Goes the seasons to each end,
at the skin, thanks to mercy
even deeper within.

Not always evergreen, but
rubicund, and gilded, and
browned to a brittle.

Goes life,
its colors, and its majesties.

We look up
and see all that rises,
all that descends.
Another new day.

November

See souls run in circles,
the leaves.
Shivery goes the air
and the trees
have tilted their heads
to spill upon their beds
and then sleep
the winter away.

Or one may think.

Instead,
underneath their blankets
of stranded tinsel
and garland there spread,
more than sticks and bones,
is the dream of sugar plums
and the bloom ahead.

See the giddy leaves run
around the eager trees
with a frolic

once thought dead.
Another new day.

December

Narrowing path below still stone in the dark cold.
You walk, not alone, but with all the tall trees.
They are barren and blunt, but are at attention.

Unseen new day sun is now seen in the barren.
Whispers of their bones, all the mighty is near.
Streak of silver garland up high metallic.
Sun behind you now lifts, mirrors itself to the wise.

Shredded balloon twisted, braided bark to bark.
Sliver of silver skin held below it, wide its banner.
Held across maybe by angels with tidings to say.
So much to say!

Wordless if not for the song of the somewhere birds.
You hear this deep within.
You hear this, as if by prayer. All of peace to share.
Another new day.

Dyed

Last Christmas, maybe just a moment ago, or forever, you died putting up the lights. Left the job unfinished. Sky burrowed deep and borrowed from our hearts our hue to darkness. And colorless bent our days, blindness blue our nights. And, now, again it's Christmas. We try our best. You help us here at the front rail where we notice the one bulb unlit. We twist on a new one, a fresh luminance. From there, we string the weathered holly you had loved so much. And soon, all the colors are once again in place, and we sense your face in all this light of Christmas.

Dresser of Sycamores

I have mine and you have yours.
We all have our calling.

Leaves go red and wrinkle.
And fall from trees.

We each can take a walking stick
for our varied little ways.

We can find heaven near Emmaus,
as we share bread.

We can find heaven in Christmas
as never meant to leave the heart.

And here we all are.
We can be found.

No matter the specter of gloom,
there is light.

No matter the darkest day or night,
there is a new bud worth the wait.

To show the way.

A Heart Is Not Plastic

Some poinsettias stay vibrant
because they are simply fake.
What is real doesn't play it safe.

There is vulnerability in change.
And faith in what shall remain,
Christmas into eternity.

Gifts for the world are wrapped.
But, faith is a fully loaded seed
far wider than just the world.

Calendar comes and goes,
and things get lost along the way.
Not what is in the heart to stay.

Treasure it within, ever genuine.
But, it is meant to be unpacked
in the same way a seed is meant

to sprout.

Soon, old things have passed.
Behold, new things have come.
See a massive tree out back.

Real as
all the miracles in your life are real.
See how faith is to be unwrapped.

Same

go the seasons,
like age to a face,
for life is change.

And even mountains move.
But what shall remain
ever the same?

Find it
embraced by grace.
And find it here in ourselves,
the ability to decorate the world
with our hearts.

Make it the stuff of love.

And then our Christmas tree,
whether a facsimile or now alive,
shall never die.

It just shows its faceted face,
as if indeed like the world
as it whirls.

All its colors.

A Moving Grove

And soon again, the world doesn't end. Soon again, there we are hand in hand. Maybe Macbeth would worry at sight of this. For him, we find it sad what he might interpret—all this marched in wood, a forecasted demise.

But for us, the arrival means yuletide.

Christmas.

It feels so good to be here again! And we gather family to march toward it, toward asphalt and sidewalk now a forest of evergreen.

We have rushed like this before, to the summer beach, the grocery store, the hospital nursery and in so many ways, to everywhere, for life is an ongoing race.

But now, this is us at the core. Pine sap fills the air flush to our hastening hearts, warmed by nearby burning barrel of whatever, as here we stop.

Seems life forever moves, but stays still long enough to hold. These trees have gloriously marched to our city and we enthusiastically embrace ours.

Arm, arm, and out! And welcome it home.

Our Tree

And you kissed me
and spun the angels in chorus.
Fresh the wintry breeze of evergreen.

Home is the everlasting breath,
the zephyr where all of forever
swirls within a snow globe.

You said yes that long ago Christmas.
And now, so many trees later,
we still have our evergreen.

Crowning the Tree

This time of the year,
despite the darkness,
is one of a beaming diadem.

See heaven enlighten
every ornament
as surrounding orbs dangle.

The star is within reach,
a welcoming
of the interwoven.

And, in front of us,
here it is, as it was.
robed in all the rainbow.

Christmas.

Symmetry

World twirls
like a ballerina in a pirouette,
this nutcracker of a fantasy,
yet real.
And upon this
we decorate ourselves.

Evanescent the disorder,
all that is hard to hold.
So much slips away,
drifts, drifts.
What remains is
some kind of grace,
at the center of the orbit,
at the core
of the aforementioned spin.

And here,
all the colors ever seen
are in place within,
all that is alive and ever was
is indeed here,
layer by layer
here, this, our family tree.

The gravity, the pull,
has us here.
All of us, with it in between,
to remain as Christmas is,

as the family roots beneath
entwine serene.
And despite all the fray
in our daily labored balance
there is equilibrium within.

Family Tree

We stay snug and look up.
The star we all can see,
if we want.
It lifts our history.

Far below, small the thread
like snow, this weave
of a newborn blanket,
simply all the ages to now.

Far above, wide the sky,
yet heaven near to us as a mirror.
It is beginning to look a lot like
Christmas.

Everywhere we turn,
how blessed is our earth.
Yes, joy to it.
So much surrounds a birth.

Birds on the Wire

We wait to awaken here upon the line
after counting the time with Saint Andrew
and our daily prayer, our routine way,
surveying the empty stable from our stair.

Cold the nights, and hardened the feather.
Soon to break, the December mourns
and the overnight tears to glisten our street,
the passing days in ages of wait in our city.

Homes lift their solitary smoke, joined.
Sparse grass is as breaking glass each day
so soon to bend to the rising sun, all as one.
Darkness eventually does give way to light.

For now, we prepare our line to the one eve.
Soon, we shall finally sing our shared song,
so soon to bend to the rising sun this earth,
for star's light that night shall fill the stable.

And then, hail and blessed be!

Sound of the Train Set

Never stuck to the nativity,
so much to see and breathe
round this big ol' monstrous tree!
It is a blessing to have eternity
as I am who I am
and make my woven way
circling this mountainous pine,
big as the world.

I wish all of the world
could feel the breeze as if a gust
of timelessness
upon this passing Georgia Pacific
as I make my way like kindness
through the mist of this sap
under this tree high as a sequoia
and breathe all that is the world.

And
if only all of you could only know
just how much
I love all of you so.

Wretched Elves Lost in Ourselves

Majesties, majesties, but meanwhile,
all of it may seem too distant to know.
Too numbing of the soul.
So goes the bitterness, the cold,
the winter wilderness no vast spectacle,
dirt in the snow, aside the fantasies,
the stark realities of this lost North Pole
of hard work, labyrinth, and little rest.

We're maybe just a broken down mess.
Sight hurts when to the inside it reflects
and lands flat at the doormat of a soul.
Sadder yet, our numbness of the missed
if soon all windows get painted black.
Ours can be darkness at noon numb.

Unless maybe somehow again outlandish
we could somehow survive instead
with childlike faith, and be big that way
and finally see the Santa we once knew,
a silliness unseen to those of us grown
with eyes now so very widely closed.

Yes, yes, love is much stronger than hate.
But we're too big to be that way childish.
Perhaps, yes, we rather be blind this way.
We settle instead for the thick smoky glass,
our own coal left upon our own cold steps.
Sight hurts when to the inside it reflects.

So it can be, unlike others here, we are
like thirsty, displaced trees, left wondering,
living still to be old in our global warming,
forgetting our youth, our vast vestibule,
forgetting our home deep in the heart.
And yet still, new, we are. Just forgetting.

Friend or Foe

We can be seemingly pure and simple
as Santa, and maybe once were,
but can now be far short of real one.
In disguise, in disgust,
no lovable jolly ol' elf is same
after selling self in the eyes.

When we look into the random face,
is it that of an imposter, or
truly a trace of the living God, or
some foe from outer space, or

just a regular everyday Joe
in tired eyes and red suit,
deserved of a second chance
at what could be called Truth?

Sadly, not always easy to tell,
even when looking into the eyes.
Harder when the eyes are multiplied.
Sometimes, it's just as well, and
maybe more safe to look away.

See how so very easy and sensible
it is to be fully grown,
and not even miss the innocence
of a childlike wait.

Perhaps, best instead to be brave.
Do best to be safe.
But, be ready to trust. And then,
unveil your own genuine face.

Dreams and Dreams

Yes, you're just another Joe,
like everyone else you know.
You've come this far.
What will the future be?

Every Josephine and
every Joseph may dream.

But it can be hard to believe.

And yet,
with a name that means
God will give,
every ordinary Joe may give in.

And wonders come to be.

So, go dream, but believe.
Allow the goodness a reality.

O, to see what you shall see.

Epiphany at the Live Nativity

Drummer Boy *had* a bubble gum ring. Got the thing earlier at Acme. But now that it was missing, he was hoping it could be properly found somewhere in the hay, and so he was quietly praying to Saint Anthony.

Wandering king stumbled out of his Chevy, still chewing a chicken wing. Sat next to an ox and the rest of this adult church group cast assembling, and got to talking about, of all things, ancient authors of ancient mystery. Said he liked reading G.K.Chesterton, some scribe of long ago old time.

"Now that was a storyteller. Yep, made his points in his stories with allegories."

Shepherds, putting on their robes hoping to look right, looked at him cross-eyed.

Joseph heard nothing of it but was still a bit jumpy instead in his role, and if others only knew they would think he had suffered insanity. After all, Joseph just a half hour before finally decided to propose. Even though he was so very broke.

"Sure was," king replied. "Brought mystery alive." And the king went on about Chesterton, as if he were his very good old friend, this author from the long, long past, a stinking ambiguity to the rest of the cast. "Always solved mystery in a perfectly ordinary way, as if truth was always here. Unknown, now found."

Diamonds are in the rough, so they say. Even in hay. The *diamond* Joe chose was surely an insult under any other gal's nose. But love knows.

King finished wing, wiped hands, positioned straight the crown in his hair. Joseph got into place with the rest, as she walked back in. And he looked at her there. He noticed again how he felt so comfortable in his pose next to her, here. In fact, Joseph knew then he felt satisfactorily stable, even financially, surrounded by the longstanding smell of hay where not long ago earlier he had proposed having found his epiphany, having picked it up suddenly seen as so obvious in all that straw like faith that surely will grow. For he felt a pure radiance as Mary positioned the choir director's infant.

She looked at Joseph and smiled wearing that bubble gum ring. No regret. Earlier she had said yes.

Drummer Boy thanked Saint Anthony, winked at Jesus, and drummed his very best.

Magi at the Door

Newly wed and brand new to neighborhood, she kept running to
mailbox their first Christmastime. "We gotta keep eye out for
Magi," with great expectation she said,
regarding arriving holiday cards to this their first address, as if
they lived somewhere beyond field and fountain, moor and
mountain.

"Fine, fine," he said, "In due time." But, he could care less
instead.

By family tradition she awaited first card with Three Kings to
place it inside high atop front door. He said, "What for?" She said
for whenever we journeyed outside or for whenever anyone
journeyed on in, hopefully an epiphany would await every her or
him. Card finally came on Christmas Eve, was hung nice and
trimmed.

First came old diminutive guy in green, being all kinds of neigh-
borly, offering flowers of all things. "Make great seeds," he said
to the husband. "Yep, yang man, welcome the seeds. Allow your
own flowers!"

Please, as if he had time for seeds. Maybe diminutive guy had
such hours. He sure didn't.

Then came sweet old lady for, of all things, yes, thyme. As if the
husband had thyme for her bland needs. Please.

Then came abrupt delivery guy probably working nuts overtime on this night of all nights, Christmas Eve. Handed him package, and asked him to sign. He did. They both managed halfhearted holiday speak and the delivery guy was on his way. Then the husband realized the package was meant for next door. Surprise! Numbskull delivery guy in rush had delivered to wrong scene.

So now he had to put on coat, boots and scarf, and take it there. Sweet old lady opened door with a wide smile, and behind her was the old diminutive guy in green. She was so very hopeful for the package, quickly opened it, and reacted with joyous relief. "Ah, see Larry, thyme flies when ordering online!"

Next thing you know, no one noticed the passing of time. The young husband had a shot of wine, some cookies, and then he straightened the star on their tree. He pleasantly realized how nice it was just to breathe. Air was fine with that now present perfect final ingredient. With thyme, the old couple could finely finish their age-old traditional recipe, a surprisingly engaging, unbelievably tasty oyster parfait. Dish of it went home where the young wife welcomed back the young husband.

And time sure does fly. Before anyone knew it, following Christmas, she and he were cuddling a bouquet sweet as sugar and spice. With Magi above the door, just right.

Like a Star in the East

Show me a sign, even though
I may be slow to see. Be patient
with me. Show me a sign, even
redundantly. More than magic.
But, big as day, and I shall know.
As if all along on my daily way,
wisdom is guiding me in grace.

Show me a sign, an obvious star
to know where you are. Heaven
opening. An Emmaus epiphany.
Please reach me, and show me.
And allow heaven to find my eyes,
no matter how shut they may be.

Bloom your fireworks like flowers.
Maybe flutter blinds like leaves
in the breeze on silver maple trees.
And I shall know. Make it be
extraordinary if not ordinary enough
so that here heaven I may find.

Heal the sick, and show me a sign,
and I shall know. Manifest a smile
aimed at me. Or even a suddenly
found frown, needing instead a
smile from me. O, to be that way wise
and not spiritually blind.

By mercy, let me behold good tidings
of great joy to all people. All of us
as family, no one a stranger.
Extraordinarily, yes, a sign,
and much, much more.
One easy to see. As love.

Yes, wrapped in swaddling clothes,
in an everyday manger. Not far.
Ever close.

Round the Advent Wreath

We often ask are we there yet?
Bethlehem, Pennsylvania.
Folks are travelling all over the world
to get there.
Or wherever home is theirs.
Gee, the traffic is terrific.

Black glass of our old Buick shimmers
shooting star.
Ours is a funicular time rolling along.
We sing, but for sure we complain
sometimes burning our candles quick.
And, yes, we often seem lost, and we are.

But really not.
We are found right here on our way.
Taking time at the rest stop to pray.
There is nothing we lack.
For here we are, yes, yes, by grace
together rolling along.

Balthasar, Melchior, and Gaspar

As for us, we took the Bethlehem route to a motor inn today under awakening sky. We prefer to drive by night and follow our star. We had spent this Sunday at a festive bazaar and bought a few things, three banjos, incense and myrrh, and loaded the car. And we were grateful afterwards for the rescued tow from a local mechanic. Long story short, we survived the dead battery setback, got some shuteye, and come sunset we will be raring to go again. Soon, it will be the big night. And, moving along, we now will have the banjos to accompany every Christmas song. Yes, we all have our will to rejoice. Even God surely has a voice as one who sings at festivals.

Rose Horizon

Today's earlier sunrise, apropos, rose pink this very Gaudete Sunday and we had wondered how different, how very much the same as every day. Maybe all the colors bend and break into themselves. Even with no room at any inn, ever big is the heart in this heavenly sent big old church with all its stained glass pane that opens the soul. In communion, there is a way humanity connects past, future, as if all's the same along the way. Hope forms a line that glistens upon us, and the way of the road opens to our readiness. Good Lord somehow is always at home here with the homeless. Yes, if needed for a reminder, soon, there's always Christmas.

Night of the Radishes

The crux of Christmas
is somewhere in this.
It is seen somewhere here in the
overgrown harvest,
our festival in Oaxaca, Mexico.
Google the pics.
Or it goes unseen, because for some
unfortunately,
some things are just too unbelievable.
At first, maybe you may look for it
carved in our local root.

Wonky-shaped and huge, not tasty.
But you might see what unites us.
And see it in the piñatas and fireworks.
And the faces.
And in the sharing of deep fried doughnuts
all covered up in succulent syrup.
We have our fill.
And then, we toss our plates for good luck,
swung over our shoulders,
all of it crashing into shattered pieces.
You may see it somewhere right here

in all the rubble.
In all the joy above any trouble.
We simply laugh and enjoy life
while the carved art radishes

make meaningful images, even nativities.
What is real—God is with us. Emanuel.
For in two days,
above the broken straw a newborn in all
has surely already brought us all together,
wrapped and rolled, nestled within our souls
long after we are old. Ever believable.

Phenomena in the Forecast

Back then, these little brothers knew so little English. Still, they were ever busy wedging into a new world word by word, no matter their lack of fluency. There was that jolly ho ho ho, the one pictured by the weatherwoman on their small TV. A live shot of something happening. Her hard to know words were second-ary to her glee of the night's miracle, the falling snowflakes out the waiting window, and Santa Claus somewhere out there on her radar. The boys peered outward.

Maybe miracles in crystal arrange themselves in this looking glass in grandeur as if ever simple, one by one this one language in the newness, as if even God is humbly one of all of us, and understands.

Yes, God understands! For miraculously, it happened, right there and then, by Popo's nativity, with the infant Jesus in heavenly peace. And maybe even Joseph and Mary quickly turned their heads to the arriving excitement.

Bàba was at the swung open door, armed with presents! Just in from John F. Kennedy. This is how they knew, beyond any TV news or hard to say words, that the so called Santa somewhere out there maybe knew enough of the world, but so did their father, to be finally even faraway here, New York City.

Layering Our Christmas

Pattycake, pattycake, baker's man,
bake me a cake as fast as you can.
And you and I will take our time
to be timeless.

Lots of history in recipe to bake a cake.
Lots of blending stories.
You're the hardest worker ever seen.
Lick batter perfectly clean.

And the whole home breathes,
high in the icing atop these mountains,
bottomless as the Black Forest cake,
for Santa's sake.

Soon, Santa will get a taste.
None will go to waste.
Yes, let this be what it is.
Preciously, deliciously, just timeless.

Dearest Santa, My Love

How do you cross the sky
the way you do?
Must take so much faith,
and lack of sleep.

It is not easy for us
to make ends meet.
Our promises, our vows,
circle likes boughs,
and our humble life, you accept,
you love,
and you know.

Look at how you wrap it all in a bow
and manage it perfectly,
so to lift smiles to this family still,
as Christmas unveils next to our tree,
crazily busy,
yet in some kind of divine serenity
unfurled.

It suddenly seems a bit like
the nearby miniature nativity,
as our cut wrapping paper spreads
like hay,
and joy to the world.

We have life, hope, and eternity.

And so goes my love for you, Santa,
far as all the miles we will travel
our shared life, and this very night
so gifted to be this way
with you.

Maker of Our Small Manger

Somewhere far away,
and yet, near as here, the world,
such a small place. For a moment,
tonight, I finally think of you.

You have spun the world yearly
of your trees, and tonight we see.
This world we share, and bond
the old and the new as now.

Your motherly hands are worn,
the baskets twined and sent wide.
And tiny manger by manger, too.
Tired and poor, you love Jesus.

Somewhere far away, yet near,
long ago, yet now, you weaved
this very nativity manger,
tonight here upon our table.

And you structured the stable
for all its cherished holy figures.
Mary and Joseph see your art,
the bend of branch and twig.

And in this precious scenery,
a child shall open eyes upon us.
Brought together, each,
far and near, to here, family.

And you, we know not.
But, somehow, we do.
The wide world is a small place.
Comfortably home.

Our thanks to God for you.

Book of Numbers

We know not
all our facts and figures.
Ongoing,
the list, ongoing.
And life upon life upon life,
we are
all numbered, each life,
the full miracle of being alive,
and, not a sparrow shall fall
unaccounted.

This is wilderness below,
and this heaven knows.
There is glory here below,
God's will be done
as it is in heaven.
For forever is in the numbers,
here in the list.
And so,
beyond any passing flight,
it happens.

We are all accounted.
Even here in our exile,
never alone.
And a chariot
shall cross the sky.
Merry Christmas to all,
and to all, a good night.

Blinking Lights

Into the cool of night we string our lights,
the strands within the evergreen and
intertwine our big dreams
ahead of morning's awakening.

We allow our souls into the grace,
through all the colors of the universe,
all of the galaxies streaming by our sides.
We are pulled to beyond time,
hearing the chorus steady and clear,
over and over.

"There is a God. There always was.
There always shall be."

And despite even the dusk of us,
fast goes the sun to rise and set
the stars to the west and yet again
another chance for life to stand still
as Christmas.

It is darkest before the awakening light,
there, at the waiting, and
perhaps we had lost an unfinished refrain
by a forgotten chorus.
How said if we allowed it to drift away
into mist, into this, our loosened strands.
We know lights come and go,
and we too drift never quite finished.

Yet, Love is always near as prayer.
For Love knows no end.

Soon morning, and yet again let us see
what shall shine for all the world.
Soon morning, and of us
what shall we find ever bright?

May it be simply Christmas.
Always here in the blur where
"There is a God. There always was.
There always shall be."

Swaddling

And then,

no other sound of might
on this silent night.

Seems, in every house
not a creature's stirring,
not even a louse.

Heads are nestled
into cozy sofa pillows
while slumberland
gets murmured yet again
with each new flake landing
without a sound.

And this silence is,
gratefully, ever sweet.

Hear tremor. Drumbeat.

Pa rum pum pum pum.

Sound of life.

Heartbeat's habit,
as if surely from heaven.

As if by that same grace
we all can just fall asleep
in such heavenly peace.

Believable

A Christmas tree
has its weight.
Life has its load,

light as a feather,
spry sure as the dawn
there rising at the horizon.

Yes, Virginia,
even on this day.
Over the shoulder
Love carries a cross.

Yes, even on
Christmas.

Another day
        has begun,
   tireless as Love,
believable as
 the new sun.

What Day Is This?

"What's to-day, my fine fellow?"

"Why, Christmas Day!"

O, for life to be a praise song!
Hail and blessed be the hour
and the moment
somewhere after the winter solstice.
And yet

somewhere as if always
in the present,
despite the past and the future
after the long night moon.

And after all that is left to live
reaches for the morning window
like a hopeful lyricist,
like an old soul
fearing all is finished in the cold,
that all the salvation of a carol
forever is forever gone
now that the birds have flown away
with everything,
only for us to find
that such is gloriously not the case.

Glory be!

For it is by mercy not too late
or too old for us to sing
after midnight in Bethlehem,
when in that hour
all stands still to forever be
all the love within all our souls,
to give the present of ourselves.

Today

Gift
after
gift
lift
to
this.

This
to
lift
gift
after
gift.

Unwrap

more than gold,
          frankincense, and myrrh,
more than any sparkly ornament
or red truck with high forehead
and robust gut,
even one loaded with candy canes
and kisses,
even one filled and refilled
with stupendous stuff,
even more than all of this.
Instead,
let us lift this gift ever glittering
from our depths—
Love.
Present tense.
This we can hold, rivet by rivet
as it connects.
We receive it, and we give it.
With it,
Love is in its truest spirit

Christmas.

Emanuel

Divine
being human.

Human being
Divine.

God loves us this much.

For God is with us.

That is the unending joy
of Christmas.

Christmas

You know beyond unbearable sadness,
a morn in the breath of myrrh.
Tell us, Child,
Who shall have been given birth?

Show us sure as day falls upon the earth,
falls upon the hyssop, the straw,
the dissipating darkness,
show us light now here for us all.

Show us Your everyday broken face,
and what grace has made of it.
Show us how, despite all hatred,
Love exists.

And as the galaxies whirl into place,
and the glaciers slide, and time drifts
to the door
ever pure, soon to melt,

soon to carry us away,
let us unwrap the present
and welcome what is present all along.
Yes, Love exists. Always is.

Child,

You are this—
from the heavens, here.

Emanuel.
Love's presence.

And so to us all, our joyous Christmas!